CATHEDRAL

CALEB LEWIS

CURRENT THEATRE SERIES

First published in 2022
by Currency Press Pty Ltd,
PO Box 2287, Strawberry Hills, NSW, 2012, Australia
enquiries@currency.com.au
www.currency.com.au
in association with State Theatre Company South Australia and Country Arts SA.

Copyright: *Cathedral* © Caleb Lewis, 2022.

COPYING FOR EDUCATIONAL PURPOSES
The Australian *Copyright Act 1968* (Act) allows a maximum of one chapter or 10% of this book, whichever is the greater, to be copied by any educational institution for its educational purposes provided that that educational institution (or the body that administers it) has given a remuneration notice to Copyright Agency (CA) under the Act.
For details of the CA licence for educational institutions contact CA, 11/66 Goulburn Street, Sydney, NSW, 2000; tel: within Australia 1800 066 844 toll free; outside Australia 61 2 9394 7600; fax: 61 2 9394 7601;
email: info@copyright.com.au

COPYING FOR OTHER PURPOSES
Except as permitted under the Act, for example a fair dealing for the purposes of study, research, criticism or review, no part of this book may be reproduced, stored in a retrieval system, or transmitted in any form or by any means without prior written permission. All enquiries should be made to the publisher at the address above.

Any performance or public reading of *Cathedral* is forbidden unless a licence has been received from the author or the author's agent. The purchase of this book in no way gives the purchaser the right to perform the play in public, whether by means of a staged production or a reading. All applications for public performance should be addressed to Mollison Keightley Management, 139 Cathedral Street, Woolloomooloo NSW 2011.

Typeset by Brighton Gray for Currency Press.
Cover image by Richard Harris.

Currency Press acknowledges the Traditional Owners of the Country on which we live and work. We pay our respects to all Aboriginal and Torres Strait Islander Elders, past and present.

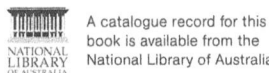
A catalogue record for this book is available from the National Library of Australia

Contents

CATHEDRAL

    Act One: Dissolution   1

    Act Two: Rapture   37

Theatre Program at the end of the playtext

Cathedral was first produced by State Theatre Company South Australia and Country Arts SA in association with Flinders University at the Space Theatre, Adelaide Festival Centre, on 6 May 2022, with the following cast:

CLAY	Nathan O'Keefe
ANGIE	Anna Steen
JOCK	Chris Pitman
KEITHEN	Arran Beatle
JESS	Annabel Matheson
WILL/TED/SUPER	Rory Walker
DJ/DEV/DAN	AJ Pate
TOPSIDE	Gavin Norris
ADITI	Sandra Anderson

Director, Shannon Rush
Set and Costume Designer, Kathryn Sproul
Lighting/Video Designer, Mark Oakley
Sound Designer/Composer, Andrew Howard
Assistant Director, Zola Allen
Production Manager, Gabrielle Hornhardt
Stage Manager, Bridget Samuel
Touring Technicians, Abbie Heuer and Tom Bayford

CHARACTERS

CLAY, a diver
JESS, a friend
POP, Clay's grandad
PILOT, a pilot
TED, a farmer
DJ, a DJ
JOCK, a commercial dive instructor
TOPSIDE, another dive student, working above water
KEITHEN, a young diver
DEV, a commercial diver
ADITI, a commercial diver
DAN, a commercial diver
ANGIE, a commercial diver; Clay's lover
SUPER, a dive superintendent

Note that in the original production Clay was the only character present on stage. All other voices were recorded.

This play went to press before the end of rehearsals and may differ from the play as performed.

ACT ONE: DISSOLUTION

SCENE ONE: CLAY AND MOSS

Warm, welcome darkness. Deep mahogany.

CLAY: The first sensation is floating.
    The second is sound.
    Voices murmuring.
    Bright gurgle
    of subterranean rivers.

Then,
a heartbeat
strong and steady,
the second smaller,
softer,
like your own.
The two of you drifting and dreaming
like castaways
on an amniotic sea.

Next comes sight,
and colour
blooms in the darkness,
softly bruising the night.
And now fingers are forming,
the two of you floating
like mirrors,
Clay and Moss,
softly bumping like buoys.

When the water breaks,
you're the first to fall,
watching your brother kick

as the umbilicus twists
and falls
round his neck
like a noose.

Then comes the push,
and the press,
and the fight,
and at last
the light.

LX: Light snaps on.

Strong hands lift you up
and a palm slaps your back,
as you suck in
deep
your first breath
until you're dizzy with air.
And already you're forgetting about your brother,
who never left the water.

SFX: A rush of tide.

SCENE TWO: THIS LIMESTONE COAST

CLAY: All of this was ocean once. This is after the split, after Gondwana cracked open and Antarctica shook off her cousins to strike out on her own. They say Australia was the last to let go. And then the great Southern Ocean swept in. And all of this—everything from Keith down through Naracoorte to Nelson got swallowed up by the flood.

That's how it started, after the coast got dunked, with those first few mussels, clams and corals come to claim it. Things would have started off small—a crab here, a few scallops—but with each new arrival, life on the reefs came to quicken. Slow creep of calcium carbonate. And every creature that carked it left its bones behind for others to build on. Strange city of otherworldly architecture, piling up and over itself, like dishes in the sink. And it's forever expanding and contracting as the sea works away at it, crumbling fine filigree, tearing loose pillars—towers rising and falling over centuries as the reef first gains then gives ground. And always there's the weight of the water pressing down on it, compacting it, while the tides push and pull at it, wearing it smooth, grinding it down.

Until the earth shifts again in its sleep, lifting the land up out of the deep to dry in the sun under a mantle of bone. That's all limestone is. This whole coast. It's haunted by a billion, billion ghosts.

We are living on bones.

SCENE THREE: 80 BAR

Liquid black.

CLAY *startles awake. A great inrush of breath!*

CLAY: Aaaaahhhhhhhhhhhh

   Then out.

Her

aah

her

aah

her

aah

her

   Shivering.
Hello?

Hello
is someone—
I can't—

If you're there
I can't see a—

A sudden burst of static.

Fuck!

Silence.

Sorry.
Scared me.

Static. Then a voice, muffled, indistinct. Static.

Say again. Over.

Static.

This is Clay. Over.

Silence.

I think I might be in trouble. Over.

Silence.

Hello?
Can you hear me?
Diver down.

Feedback!

I can't—
This isn't fucking funny!

A girl's laughter.

Then,
silence.

Jess?
Is that you?

SCENE FOUR: NIGHT SWIMMING

CLAY: We take Mum's car. Slip the keys off the hook, shutting the door behind us, then stealing down the steps, key open the car door, unkey the club-lock, release the parking brake, put her in reverse and wheel her down the driveway and out onto the road, only starting the engine once we're sure we're clear.

ACT ONE

SFX: Engine starting up. Car radio starts. Coldplay, 'Yellow'.

JESS: Coldplay?
CLAY: It's Mum's.

CLAY *switches it off.*

We drive out to the lookout, but there are others with the same idea, and tonight is ours alone. It's almost one and the air is thick with heat, the storm yet to break. We lean forward from hot vinyl seats, as sweat trickles down our backs, legs shimmering under streetlight. We drive out to Brown, drinking port from the cask, and talk about what we'll do after school as lightning crackles the horizon. And the water is smooth as stone, only Jessie's scared of sharks. She says they never stop moving, even if they wanted to, even at night, they can't rest, or they'll die.

JESS: Do you want to talk about it?
CLAY: Nup.

Key the ignition, nose the car inland, and head out to the pics, roos flickering in the headlights. We double back along eight-mile creek, turn down Tillers, then Glenelg River road, headed for Nelson, until we hit the turnoff, and swing south again, back towards the coast, breathing it in, trading asphalt for gravel as we ease the car forward through saltbush and scrubland and sedge.

The ponds are a natural cave system: limestone dredged up from the seabed and hollowed out by rainwater over thousands of years. They sit behind sand dunes, so close they could kiss the coast, yet the water is clean and bright as gin. Pull into the empty car park and then we're out the car and dashing down the path, tripping in our haste as we cast off clothes— and then there's the jetty, and we're laughing, leaping, shrieking, like little kids again, as we spill from the sky into water. And for a moment it resists us, and we hang suspended over a mirror of stars—and then the surface dimples and breaks, and then we're through.

Gasps.

The pond is a cold, bright slap. Hear Jess shriek as the shiver runs right through us.

JESS: Close your eyes.

CLAY: And then her lips brush mine

    CLAY *reaches out for her.*
JESS: Nuh uh uh.

CLAY: And she moves away from me, somewhere close, only just out of—

JESS: Polo.
CLAY: What?
JESS: Polo.
CLAY: Jess?
JESS: Polo!
CLAY: Marco?
JESS: … Polo.
CLAY: Marco.
JESS: … Polo.
CLAY: Marco.
JESS: [*whispered*] Open your eyes.

CLAY: She floats like a crocodile.

JESS: Here.

CLAY: Her bra!

JESS: Don't lose it.

CLAY: But when I reach out to—she's already duck diving under, then surfacing, just out of reach.
    I follow, until we're out over the chasm where it's deepest.
    The two of us tread water, neither speaking, and when I reach this time, she doesn't pull away. We cling to one another under a busted moon, this desperate tangle of limbs, and each time we're right on the precipice—

JESS: Wait—
> *She laughs.*

CLAY: And it's only when we've almost drowned four times that we manage to pull ourselves apart and paddle back towards the jetty. Then something—

What?
JESS: I felt something.
CLAY: I hope so.
JESS: I'm serious! Something brushed my—
> *A splash.*

What was that?
CLAY: Just a duck or something.
JESS: Let's go.
CLAY: Unless …
JESS: What?
CLAY: It could be a *bonefish*?
JESS: What's a bonefish?
CLAY: Like a tank with teeth.
JESS: Is that right?
CLAY: They ruled the ocean for millions of years.
JESS: You're such a boy.

CLAY: She kicks away, splashing water in my face.

JESS: Well?
CLAY: Well what?
JESS: Seduce me, you idiot.

CLAY: When she climbs the ladder, her knickers are pale blue. I slip a finger inside the elastic, tugging gently as she pulls away, slipping them down past her hips, then her knees as she sighs, leaning back against me—

JESS: Stop.
CLAY: What's wrong?
JESS: Someone's here.
CLAY: There's nobody—
JESS: Shhh!
CLAY: We woulda heard their car.
JESS: I can see their stuff!
CLAY: … What stuff?
JESS: [*calling out*] Hello?
CLAY: What stuff?
JESS: Is someone there?
CLAY: Jess?
JESS: Shoes.
CLAY: Where?
JESS: And, see, clothes
    And a handbag as well.
CLAY: What's it look like?
JESS: [*calling out again*] Hello?! Is someone / here?
CLAY: We should go.
JESS: Now?
CLAY: Let's go.
JESS: But what about—
CLAY: Leave it.
JESS: I'm just checking for—
CLAY: Put it down.
JESS: We have to tell someone.
CLAY: Put it down. We have to go.
JESS: In a second.
CLAY: NOW!
JESS: Clay? What's wrong?
CLAY: The bag.
    It's my mum's.

SCENE FIVE: POP

CLAY: Pop taught me to swim. This was just after Dad left. After Pop saw the bruises round mum's neck and he and Dad had a word. He found Dad at Flanagan's, kicked the stool out from under him and dragged him out onto the street. Dad was mean but Pop was relentless. Took his belt off and flogged him bloody in front of half the town. Police never pressed charges. Pop was a war hero. He came back that night, fists swollen and hanging heavy like cinderblocks. Mum sent me down the Caltex for a bag of ice and by the time I got back she was almost done screaming at him. I waited out front till she was done then put the ice in the freezer.

We never saw Dad again after that. Pop'd pick me up after school and take me down the pool to run laps with the kickboard. By then I was almost thirteen, twice as tall as the other kids, but Pop didn't give a shit. And only after I'd finished a dozen laps would he set aside the form guide, strip down to his speedos and join me. We'd start out treading water, then it was freestyle, then breaststroke. Pop had no time for style, only competence. Everything he did was deliberate. We'd finish off at the bottom of the pool, holding onto our breath and the ladder until spots swam in my eyes. That last bit was my favourite, down there at the bottom with Pop, holding on to the ache until I'd almost pass out, knowing Pop was with me and would never let go. After swimming he'd buy me a bucket of chips soaked in vinegar and have me home in time for dinner—don't tell your mum.

Once Pop was happy I could hold my own in the pool, we started heading out to Racecourse Bay. Pop taught me to bodysurf, and we spent almost every morning in the sea until my skin was brown as beer nuts and crusted in salt. When I turned fourteen Pop bought my first wetsuit. That summer I was up every morning with the dawn, waiting for the honk of Pop's truck. Then it was fifteen minutes to the beach, another five to wrestle on our wetsuits, wade out between the waves and—splash!

By the time I was sixteen, we'd started to drift a bit. I'd cancel one weekend than the next, and Pop would head out on his own while I nursed another hangover. Mum wasn't stupid, but she had her own stuff to deal with, and I guess understood what Pop couldn't—that boys outgrow their grandads—even Moss, who'd never been born. Besides, Pop was getting on. The arthritis played hell on his hands and I watched him grit his teeth every time he hit the water. In a way I was doing him a favour. Things between us might have ended right there if it weren't for what happened with Mum. After that he took me / in—

SCENE SIX: 55 BAR

A sudden burst of static.

CLAY: Hello?

The static is ongoing now, a constant low-level whisper.

Is anyone—

CLAY *listens, but it's silent. He waits ... Nothing. Then—is that music?*

Hello?

Can you hear—

And then a voice: discernible, but illegible.

WILL: [*static*] Come in [*static*] over.

CLAY *presses his underwater comms.*

CLAY: This is Clay. Diver down. Over.
WILL: [*static*]
CLAY: Say again—
PILOT: [*static*]
CLAY: Sorry?
I don't under—
PILOT: [*static*] Mayday [*static*]
CLAY: Come in. Over.

But the static is roaring now, like wind through a tunnel. The music, jangled and discordant.

Hello? I can't hear you. Over. Come in?

The static grows louder, like a raging fire, like a storm, drowning everything out except the engine and the flak and the plane falling out of the sky.

SCENE SEVEN: BLUE DANUBE

CLAY: 1944. Pop's not even a dad yet. One day he'll be a tough old bastard, and raise me up as his own, but right now he's just a kid, not yet twenty, knuckles white, eyes squinted tight, as the plane drops out of the sky.

The pilot is fighting the wheel, but he might as well fight gravity. One engine is on fire, the other has stalled, and somewhere someone is screaming. And huddled in his seat, Pop would have had a front-row seat as the earth rushed up to greet him. Legs braced, head between his knees, as though it might somehow save him, and then the shock when the bomber hits the water.

They are in the Danube, which is not bloody blue, but cold and dark and getting darker as the propeller pulls them down. And as one by one the lights blink out and the water surges in, it's only now he thinks back to the summer spent in Brighton and wishes he'd learned to swim. See him struggling with his belt, but already his fingers are numb, shoulder shot, as the last bright pocket of air burps its way out. By twisting his head and extending his neck at an angle he steals one last breath—then clamps his mouth shut as the water laps his lips. And in a way, it's easier now, the water calmer, now it's got him. He slows his hands, works the belt loose by touch, with fingers so numb they might as well be someone else's. Until—click—and he's free.

As the seatbelt falls away, he pulls himself up inside the fuselage, more like a silo now, inside the vertical plane. High above, the bomb bay doors are open and he catches a glimpse of starlight and kicks towards it, arm hanging deadweight, up past floating cargo, and bodies, and unexploded bombs, and he's almost out now, so close he can touch the sky, then something grips him by the ankle and yanks him down.

A loose strap.
The plane trailing dozens as it dives.
Ribbons unfurling like streamers
intestine

from the disembowelled bomber.
This is it
he thinks.
It won't let me go.
He cries out then
any stoicism left in him
leaving him
and as his eyes roll back in his head
catch movement
from below.

***

Later
when he's up on his own
after Joan and the kids have gone to bed
he'll try to remember
who
or what it was
that saved him.
Pale fingers
loosing the strap round his ankle.
Cold, wet skin
carrying him up into the light.
And eyes blue
like his own.

SCENE EIGHT: BLACKWATER

CLAY: Anyone tells you the first days are the hardest is lying. Not out of malice, but only to hold back a truth from you they think you don't yet know. That this pain will last forever. That some things can't be ducked, or shared, or shouldered by others, and can only be endured.

    Jessie held out as long as she could then left for uni in Adelaide. I didn't blame her. She had her own life to lead and all I could offer now was silence broken only by the burble of the bong. Nights I'd play pool at Tarpeena or head out to the lighthouse ruins at Cape

Northumberland and fish for snapper off the rocks. I'd hang right out on the edge in the spray, listening to the wind howl and the gulls shriek, daring the sea to come smash me away. There was a steel kind of comfort in it. It was the only place that matched how I felt. Come sunrise, I'd bag the night's catch or head home empty-handed. The fish didn't matter. Most night the hooks weren't even baited.

After the house sold, I moved into Pop's. I didn't bring much with me. A few rods, some CDs—Mum's—and a half ounce of weed. Pop hardly seemed to notice. Still lost in his own world of grief. After the second week, with the dishes piling up, and the whole house stinking of dope, he found my gear and tossed it. When I barked, he bit, and when I swung at him, he roared. The two of us twisted up on the rug in this snarl of rage. Later, I started on the dishes and Pop started drying. Looking back, I should have cut him more slack. It wasn't just me who was suffering. He'd lost his own little girl.

Come December she'd been gone a whole year and we still hadn't talked about it. I took a job in the pines through Aunty Kim and lasted almost a month. After that I got by on the dole and cash-in-hand jobs with Pop. Bill was a handyman. He had a knack for fixing things that others would have chucked. End of winter we were up to our elbows in work. The rains had finally let up but all the local paddocks had gone to bog. The cattle had survived it, clumping together on any ridge or rise they could find, but flash flooding had swept through the scrub, picking up a year's worth of leaf litter plus two or three calves and dumped the lot in Mitchell's dam. A week later, the sun is out and the dam is fouled up like a truck stop toilet. Fertiliser runoff. It makes everything richer and sweeter and somehow more wrong. You can feel it crawl up your nostrils, and roll around in your mouth. Maybe it was the hangover or knowing what was coming, but I swear you could smell it from the highway and by the time I had my mask on I was ready to gag. Problem was Pop had done his back. He'd already cleared out most the mulch, but he needed me to go down and haul out the calves. A hundred bucks—which felt like a lot last night, but looking at it now …

TED: [*laughing*] Better you than me kid.

CLAY: Ted Mitchell winks at me. Two Vicks inhalers up his nose and beaming like a walrus.

    I tie the rope round my waist, slide down the bank on my arse and wade in. Mud squelches between my toes and the water sloshes like cold coffee. Soon I'm up to my chest, then my neck, and then there's nothing left but to do but dive.

    I take a breath, give Ted the finger, and plunge.

The vis is bad.
Water black as tea from all the tannins and full of slop.
My eyes are open,
but it's useless,
the dam thick as gravy,
have to feel my way by touch.
This is.
Gross.
    …
Find the first calf easy,
head trapped in a snag,
body floating
like a velvet balloon.
Slip the rope round its neck,
tie it tight
then tug for the others to haul.
Find the second,
but its stomach's already split.
We get it out in one piece
by the skin of its hide
and then I'm diving for the third
when her fingers touch mine.

    SFX: An eruption of bubbles.

Feel the water hit the back of my throat.
Try to
kick

for the surface—
Fuck!
But all I do is stir up silt.
Watch it float up towards me
big yellow cloud.
Lungs sucking water.
Fight it.
Can't find the surface.
Find it!
But the water won't let go.
Thrashing now
in mud
and blood
and—

A great gasp of air.

Pop drags me out.
Hauls me up on to the bank
And leaves me gasping in the—

Mum!
   He stops.
She's down there.

See the fight in his eyes.
Hope and logic.

It's her.
After.

After the cops have left and the dam's been dredged.
He can't look at me.

I saw her.

I know you think you did.
I know I did.

You need to go, he says.
Where?
Any place but here.

SCENE NINE: 30 BAR

Blackout.

CLAY: Shivering.
  Never felt cold like this.
  Got to keep—
    SFX: An echo.
  Who's there?
    Beat.
  Get a grip.
  Just the nitrogen talking.
  Start listening to that and it's over.
  Concentrate.
  Remember the drill.
    CLAY *reaches for his torch.*
  Torch is gone.
  Doesn't matter.
  Find the line and then—
  Fuck!
  Don't panic.
  Don'tpanicdon'tpanicdon'tpanicdon'tdeepslowbreathsdeepslow-breathsdeepslowbreaths
  Deepslowbreaths
  deepslowbreaths
  Deep slow breaths
  Deep
  Slow
  Breaths.
  Deeeeep
  Sloooow
  Better.

…
Now.
…
Check your spare.

CLAY feels around in the dark. It's not good news.

That's okay.
No need to panic. Not yet.
Remember the drill.

CLAY snaps a glowstick. A tenuous circle of light.

Always have a backup.

He holds it up to his reg.

Depth is …
Can't be right.
Shake it.
Check again.
But the needle insists.
Ninety metres.
Pressure at thirty bar.
Which means the tank is almost—
Aaargh!

Picks up a splinter.

Is that
bone?
What is this place?
Where the fuck am I?

SCENE TEN: KOH PHA NGAN

Electronic dance music (something like Da Rude's 'Sandstorm').

We watch CLAY's body go limp as the pills take hold. He begins to dance, slow at first, then faster, matching the beat with amphetamine focus, waving the glowstick in the air. A voice echoes through the darkness.

DJ: This is your captain speaking.

The crowd and CLAY *roar.*
Koh Pha Ngan, make some noise.
The crowd and CLAY *roar louder.*
Louder.
The crowd and CLAY *roar louder.*
Who wants to get fucked up?
CLAY *and the crowd roar, 'YES!'*
Welcome. To. Oblivion!
The song drops and the stage explodes in rapid bursts of laser light.

Later.
Sunrise.
The light warm and intense.
Waves lap at the shore.
CLAY *shields his eyes.*

CLAY: Barely sunup and it's already thirty.
Wake sprawled in a deckchair.
Sand in my hair.
My eyes.
My arse.

Time is it?
I feel like a dog shat in my head.
Freya? Got any water?
JOCK: Wake up son.
CLAY: What?
JOCK: You're swimming in it.

CLAY: Sit up. See this old bloke, must be forty, skin red like a roasted tomato.

JOCK: Who's Moss?
CLAY: What?

ACT ONE

JOCK: You were having a nightmare.
CLAY: Where's Freya?
JOCK: She left.
CLAY: Shit.
JOCK: Took your wallet as well.
CLAY: You didn't stop her?!
JOCK: I'm not your mum.

CLAY: Get up to go.

JOCK: This yours?

CLAY: *He holds up a baggie of pills.*

Thanks.
JOCK: How long you been here?
CLAY: Three years.
JOCK: So why are you still acting like a tourist?
CLAY: … It's a free country.
JOCK: If they catch you with this shit—
CLAY: I know.
I just needed a little help last night.
It was an anniversary.
JOCK: Not yours and Freya's, I'm guessing.
CLAY: Piss off.
JOCK: Here.

CLAY catches the bag, starts to leave.

What's the hurry?
CLAY: I have to teach.
JOCK: English?
CLAY: Diving.
JOCK: Snorkel or—
CLAY: SCUBA.
JOCK: Good man.
CLAY: You dive?
JOCK: On occasion.

CLAY: You should come out to the reef. See the clownfish.
JOCK: You on commission?
CLAY: I'll do you mate's rates.
JOCK: Cheeky cunt.
CLAY: But his face cracks a smile.
JOCK: Save it for the tourists.
CLAY: You don't know what you're missing.
JOCK: Are you happy here?
CLAY: Why wouldn't I be?
JOCK: That out there, it's a bathtub.
Fun for a dip, but if I had to sit in it all day, I'd slit my wrists. When you've had your fill of clownfish come see me in Scotland and I'll show you a real ocean.
CLAY: ... Okay.
JOCK: Fucking clownfish.

SCENE ELEVEN: ABERDEEN

Blackout.

TOPSIDE: [*voiceover*] Stick is hot.

LX: A small flare of dazzling white light in front of CLAY.

CLAY: Strike the arc and watch a star burn underwater, hold it steady as I work the stick down the puddle, keep the light dancing on the end of the stinger.

Make it cold.

LX: The light dies.

TOPSIDE: [*voiceover*] Stick is cold.

CLAY: Job is a routine wet-weld—switching out burned-out anodes on a steel plate. Saltwater eats everything, especially metal. Leave it down there long enough and the sea will take it all.

Make it hot.

LX: The flare lights up.

TOPSIDE: [*voiceover*] Stick is hot.

CLAY: There's eight of us working in pairs. Four in the water, the others topside, tending hoses and working the switch.

> Make it cold.
> *LX: The flare goes out.*

TOPSIDE: [*voiceover*] Stick is cold.

CLAY: The star blinks out and the water stops fizzing. I lower the stick to check the join—not bad—then see how the others are doing. It's not a race, but no-one wants to come last. Baahir's on his last weld: clean, steady lines, same as me—but when I turn to check on Keithen, the kid gives me the finger, fumbles, and drops the stinger like a mic right onto his wrist.

> Diver down!

Push towards him but the suit moves like a dreadnought. Baahir shoves past, hose tangling with mine, as the kid twitches like a Tickle-me-Elmo. Then someone hits the knife-switch and his body goes limp.

> Go!

Try to grab him but the suit hangs deadweight. Drag him back to the ladder, umbilicals twisting, just as the kid starts coming round.

> Keithen?

He flinches, faceplate splashed with sick.

> Keithen, it's me.

His eyes flutter like moths behind the glass.

You've had a shock mate.

And then they're wide and full of fear.

Stay calm. We're gonna get you out of—

But the kid is having none of it.

Keithen, stop!

And for a second I think I got through to him.
Then he drops his weights
and rockets to the surface.

***

JOCK: You stupid fucks.
   Which one of you want to tell me what happened?

CLAY: Jock squats by the pool, fury compacted into a tight ball of rage.

JOCK: Well?

CLAY: There's eight of us. A couple of ex-navy, and the rest are strays like me. Two Scots and a Pom, one Filipino, two Israelis, a Somali and me. Mostly young guys with no commitments who heard about the money you could make. It took six years to get here—four bumming round Europe—then when the money ran out, a coach to Edinburgh and two years dish-pigging to save up for the course. When I finally got here, the first thing Jock says to me—

JOCK: You took your time.

CLAY: This is our first month in Aberdeen. We started on SCUBA to thirty metres, then SSBA. Last week was lightweight and rigging. Up next is offshore and hazmat; salvage; then decompression dives using wet bells, hot suits and gas. We're supposed to finish with a deep dive, but given Jock's current mood …

ACT ONE 23

JOCK: Not fucking likely.

CLAY: It's been almost twenty minutes. The three of us are still in the water, helmets off, weighed down with weights, suits and harnesses, but no-one's getting out yet.

JOCK: Take your time lads, I can wait all day.

CLAY: Both arms are numb. I try to focus on the tiles in front of me. Watch the water lap at them and limn them. Push past the cramp in my legs and the sparks in my lungs.

JOCK: Keithen.
KEITHEN: Yes Jock.
JOCK: Do you enjoy shitting yourself?
KEITHEN: No Jock.
JOCK: Some kind of auto-erotic thing?
KEITHEN: It was an accident.
JOCK: YOU WERE SHOWING OFF! Waving that stick around like a fucking lightsaber and look what happened!

CLAY: I watch the veins in his temple flicker.

JOCK: And you two. Was that a rescue or a clown show, because I can't tell? If that sideshow had gone down in the Atlantic instead of a swimming pool, all three of you would be dead, and there'd be no-one else to blame. Are you listening?
CLAY: Yes Jock.
JOCK: Down there, everything is on you. No, you look at me! Embolisms; hypothermia; hypoxia; pneumo-thorax; barotrauma. Every time you enter the water you take your life in your hands. And the deeper you go, / the greater the risk.
CLAY: The greater the risk.

The kid is struggling, chin just above water but Jock's not having a bar of it. Reach out to—

JOCK: Leave him.
CLAY: But Jock—
JOCK: I said let him go.
CLAY: He'll drown.
JOCK: That's up to him.
 And you can forget all that Jacques Cousteau shit—especially you Nemo. No-one's getting paid to dive with dolphins at sunset, you're here to toil in the great cold dark.

CLAY: None of us are listening. All eyes on Keithen as he slips beneath the surface.

JOCK: Diving is the vehicle not the job. All this is just how you get there. So, if by some miracle, any of you pass this course and make it as a commercial diver, you can kiss the sky goodbye. Instead, you'll be slaving on the seabed, maintaining million-dollar infrastructure so that others who are smarter and warmer get their annual cunting bonus.
CLAY: Fuck this
JOCK: Clay, stop!

CLAY: Then Keithen's hands find the ladder and all of us start cheering as he pulls himself up, rung by rung, head breaking the surface like a promise, gasping for breath.

JOCK: Are you listening?
 There's a reason this job is so well paid. It's called hazard pay.

CLAY: The kid clings to the ladder like a barnacle.

JOCK: How much did you drink last night?
KEITHEN/CLAY: None Jock.
JOCK: I can smell the whisky on your breath.
 Well?
 Get the fuck out of my pool.

CLAY: Jock heads for his office while the others give Keithen a hand.

JOCK: A death wish? Is that it.

CLAY: No Jock.

JOCK: You can get blind enough down there, riding the rapture, without bringing your own bottle to the party. I mean, who needs Talisker, we've got nitrogen, baby! Dive at pressure, let that shit dissolve in your blood and BAM you're mainlining God. First comes laughter, then terror, then the pink elephants! You might think you're top shit up here, but the deep doesn't care. Down there, you're just another tadpole in the dark.

SCENE TWELVE: 15 BAR

CLAY *lies prone at the bottom of the abyss, his body convulsing, then twitching, then still.*

...

A minute passes.

...

Another.

...

A sudden gasp.

SCENE THIRTEEN: NORTH SEA

DEV: [*high-pitched*] Suck it up lads!

CLAY: Dev slams his cards down on the table, triggering howls of protest from Dan and Aditi, and calls to 'shut the fuck up' from those of us trying to sleep. The whole can is in uproar, but Dev is impervious; Cheetos bounce off his forehead. Day nine and we're already sick of each other. Eight sardines in the can plus four in the bell. Check my watch. Four hours until I'm back in the water. Then three weeks until home.

ADITI: [*high-pitched*] Another game?

CLAY: Listen to the riffle of cards under Alessandro snoring. Angie's reading; Martin's shaving in the wet pot; and Keithen's taking selfies. Witness the glamour of commercial deep diving. When we're not freezing our tits off at the bottom of the ocean, you can find us in here, doing time in a pressurised tank. Before saturation, divers spent more time in the bell than they did on the bottom. Might only take minutes to get down there but coming back up could take hours and a dozen deco stops unless you were planning to pop. Then someone figured out, if they just kept us under pressure, they wouldn't have to decompress us until the end of the job. It's an inconvenience, sure, but the money's insane and all it costs us are these great bouts of boredom, and the knowledge that the slightest breach will kill us on the spot. Strange sort of life. I've spent whole nights on the seabed humming along to dolphin song, and whole days in silence here after every joke's been told and every book's been read. Commercial diving's a paradox, see. You're never alone, yet you'll never feel lonelier. Job's the most isolated in the world. You can bring astronauts home faster than deep sea divers. It takes four hours to bring someone back from space. The wait for divers in deco is days at a minimum.

KEITHEN: [*high-pitched*] Can I borrow your hot sauce?
CLAY: Sure.

Something I might not have mentioned is the heliox. It's a mix of helium and oxygen which they sub in on sat dives. The result is a tincan full of tough guys who all sound like Elmo. All of us adjust pretty quick, but the accents don't make it easy. Glaswegians are tough to make out at the best of times. Try turning up the treble to eleven.

KEITHEN: [*high-pitched*] Thanks pal, you're a star.

CLAY: Dan slumps in the bunk below Ange, reading a magazine and sucking on a Vapodrop. He's not sick—if he was, they wouldn't let him dive—but the man is terrified of blocked ears or sinuses. A cold down here can end a career. Every one of us is a mobile pharmacy.
    Steal another glimpse at Angie. She sits, back against the bulkhead, Kindle balanced on her knees. She gets this look, when

ACT ONE

she concentrates, tiny kink in her brow like an upside-down tick. She looks up, eyebrows arched and my eyes duck away, feigning interest in the rivets by my bed. Count to ten and look back to see her smiling, and even if the air we breathe is doctored, the chemistry is undeniable.

She shifts in her bunk, letting her singlet slip off one shoulder, and I'm gobsmacked. It's been like this for days now. What she's doing is cruel and the fact she knows it only makes it all the sweeter. She stares back at me, faint smile on her lips. It's been two days since she jumped me in the wet pot, boldly took the toothbrush out my mouth and slipped her tongue in. The taste of toothpaste and—

SFX: Loud knocking.

CLAY: [*muttering*] Fuck.
KEITHEN: [*high-pitched*] Hurry up, I have to take a shit.

CLAY: Now lust is a resilient thing, but there are certain phrases—

KEITHEN: [*high-pitched*] My arse is gonna burst.

CLAY: Angie pulls away, dabs toothpaste from my chin, and saunters out. That was forty-nine hours ago. Just five hundred to go.

DAN: [*high-pitched*] Clay?
CLAY: Yeah?
DAN: [*high-pitched*] Do you know this place?

CLAY: Dan holds up the dive mag, pointing at a photo of the ponds.

DAN: [*high-pitched*] You ever been here?

    CLAY *nods.*

[*High-pitched*] Says here they've got some of the best dives in the world.
KEITHEN: [*high-pitched*] Why'd you leave?
DAN: [*high-pitched*] On account of all the sinkholes, see. Whole place is riddled with them.

KEITHEN [*high-pitched*]: Clay?
DAN [*high-pitched*]: See, this one's Iddlebiddy.
KEITHEN [*high-pitched*]: Clay?
DAN: [*high-pitched*] And that's tank cave. They still haven't mapped it all yet.
And that's—
CLAY: The cathedral.
Beat.
DAN: [*high-pitched*] Ever dive it?
CLAY: … no.
KEITHEN: [*high-pitched*] Why not?
DAN: [*high-pitched*] Says here, there's bodies still down there.
People who got lost and never found their way out.
KEITHEN: [*ghost noises*] Ooooooohooooohoooooh

CLAY: Shove Keithen hard against the wall, my hands at his throat. The whole tank silent now except for Keithen choking.

ANGIE: Clay?
CLAY: Angie?
ANGIE: Let him go.
SFX: A dive watch alarm.
CLAY: Nod.
Watch him drop to the floor.

SCENE FOURTEEN: 10 BAR

CLAY: Check the watch.
It's been …
Dunno.
Glass is cracked.
Check my air.
Ten bar left.
Wait till five
Then—
Suck it.

Hold.
Gas off.
Detach tank
and
switch to the pony.
Gas on.
Breathe.
Then wait for the needle to rise.
Five.
Ten.
The needle stalls at twenty.
Oh.
I thought there'd be more.
Not long now.
Look around,
but there's nothing to see

I read a book once.
Not a lot to do in the tank.
Anyway, this book
it was on dying
and how we've got it all wrong.
How death's not life's end
but its absence.
Like a shadow.
It's nothing on its own
there's nothing there.
It's just the absence of light.

Hands are numb.
Body so cold it hurts.
I miss the sun and the sand.
Even sunburn is better than this.
Shoulda brought a thicker wetsuit
and a thermos
and a bucket of chips soaked in—
Everything

slows down
and softens then.
Hands.
Even the stars.
Watch them
drip down
like bird shit
from above.

It splashes CLAY's *shoulder.*

ANGIE: Oh no!
CLAY: Angie?
ANGIE: Ah well, they say it's good luck.

SCENE FIFTEEN: HULL

Humber Bridge, Hull. The sound of seagulls. CLAY *and* ANGIE *hover high above the water.*

ANGIE: I've been dying for this.
CLAY: Sorry?
ANGIE: Best blood sausage in England.
CLAY: Right?
ANGIE: You don't know what you're missing.

CLAY: She grins, bright gobs of purple staining her teeth.

ANGIE: Best thing about leaving the can is getting your tastebuds back.
CLAY: I'll take your word.
ANGIE: Fuck yeah!
CLAY: Thanks for asking me here.
ANGIE: The bridge?
CLAY: Hull.
ANGIE: No bother.
CLAY: …
ANGIE: I'll take you by the chippy later. The one where the lassie bit this fella's tongue off in a fight and a seagull ate it up like a chip.
CLAY: You don't have to entertain me.

ACT ONE

ANGIE: I've already hired the band!
CLAY: I mean I'm good on my own.
ANGIE: But you're better with me.

CLAY: Stand up on my tiptoes, looking down at the water.

ANGIE: So … anyone back home I should know about?
CLAY: …
ANGIE: I just want to know what we're doing.
CLAY: I haven't been back in years.
ANGIE: Why not?
CLAY: The blood sausage. It's terrible.
ANGIE: What was that about with Keithen?
    I mean, he's a twat, I get it, but you know the kid idolises you.
CLAY: How high up are we?
ANGIE: There's a barrier.
CLAY: What?
ANGIE: If you were thinking of jumping.
CLAY: What? No!
ANGIE: I'll take *that* as a compliment.
CLAY: … Do you get many?
ANGIE: Compliments?
CLAY: Jumpers?
ANGIE: One or two a month.
CLAY: Jesus.
ANGIE: More in the winter.
    This is before the plexiglass. Now it's down to a trickle.
CLAY: … Do any survive?
ANGIE: From here?
    See down there, by the pylon. That's where I found my first body.
CLAY: First?
ANGIE: People think it's quick, that's it's over the instant you hit the water, but the body falls too fast, see, so when it does hit, it hammers right through.
    That's how we'd find them, playing stuck in the mud.
CLAY: …

ANGIE: The thing that always got me was the shoes. Each time we fished a body out, one of us would look up here after. And you'd find all kinds of things. Umbrellas, keys, a coat neatly folded. But it was the shoes that got me.

CLAY: Why?

ANGIE: They didn't want to get them wet.

    Beat.

CLAY: I found hers
   on the jetty.
   My mum's.
   After the (accident).
   At least
   I think
   that's what happened.
   She could have just left.
   Caught a greyhound.
   We never held a funeral
   I mean
   they never found a body.
   …
   She used to kiss me on the eyelids
   at night
   when she'd tuck me in.
   Every night
   until …
   I hope she's happy.
   I do.
   Because if she's not.
   I mean if she didn't skip town
   that means she's still down there
   underneath the cathedral.

SCENE SIXTEEN: THE BELL

Blackout.

SFX: Alarm. A flashing amber light.

CLAY, *alone in the water. We hear him communicate with* ANGIE, *working tender in the second dive bell, and the* SUPER *on the vessel above.*

ANGIE: [*distortion*] Come in. Over.

    Beat.

  Bell two to diver one. Come in. Over.

DSV: [*distortion*]

ANGIE: Clay?

SUPER: [*distortion*] requesting update. Over.

ANGIE: [*distortion*]

SUPER: [*distortion*] Say again. Over.

ANGIE: [*distortion*]

SUPER: [*distortion*] confirm diver status. Over

ANGIE: [*distortion*] not fucking answering.

CLAY: [*distortion*] Diver one to Bell two. Over.

ANGIE: Clay?

CLAY: Breaking up. Over.

ANGIE: It's the storm. Over.

CLAY: [*distortion*]

ANGIE: Clay, it's a mess up there.

    I don't know how much longer we can stay down here. Over.

CLAY: …

ANGIE: Clay?

CLAY: Still no sign. Over.

ANGIE: Honey? I know you want to help them. Over.

CLAY: …

ANGIE: They were my friends too.

CLAY: [*distortion*] something.

ANGIE: Clay?

CLAY: I've found them. Over.

ANGIE: Oh thank Christ.

Bell two to DSV [*distortion*]. Diver has sighted bell one. Over.
SUPER: [*distortion*] thank fuck. Requesting coordinates. Over.
ANGIE: Sending now. Over.
SUPER: [*distortion*] Over.
ANGIE: Clay?
CLAY: ...
ANGIE: Clay?
CLAY: ...
ANGIE: Clay come in?
CLAY: [*distortion*] on the sea bottom [*distortion*] Umbilical is shorn right through.
ANGIE: Oh Christ.
CLAY: [*distortion*] bell appears intact.
ANGIE: And the lads? Confirm diver status. Over.
CLAY: [*distortion*]
ANGIE: Say again. Over.
CLAY: They're alive. Over.
ANGIE: Yes!
CLAY: [*distortion*] I can see [*distortion*] waving at the window [*distortion*] Isaiah.
ANGIE: And Keithen?
CLAY: [*distortion*] Holding a note up. Hang on.

He laughs.

ANGIE: What?
CLAY: He wants to know who won the football?
ANGIE: [*laughing*] Little shit. I tell you that boy's got more lives than a cat! Over.
SUPER: [*distortion*]
ANGIE: Bell two to DSV say again. Over.
SUPER: Immediate evac [*distortion*]
CLAY: Approaching the drop-weight now. As soon as it's released, and the bell is loose, I'll send the boys on their way. Over.
ANGIE: Clay?
CLAY: ...
ANGIE: Bell two to diver one. Over.
CLAY: [*distortion*]

ACT ONE   35

ANGIE: Come in. Over. Bell two to diver one.
　　SFX: intense feedback.
　Clay, come in. Over.
　　Clay?
CLAY: Weight is jammed. Over.
ANGIE: [*distortion*]
CLAY: I can't detach it.
ANGIE: [*distortion*]
CLAY: Angie?
SUPER: [*distortion*] conditions deteriorated [*distortion*] immediate evac. Over.
ANGIE: Clay?
　　They want us to—
　　The storm's got worse
　　We have to go.
　　Clay?
　　Clay, come in?

SCENE SEVENTEEN: AFTER

ANGIE: Clay?
CLAY: Mum?
ANGIE: Wake up sleepyhead.
CLAY: Ange?
ANGIE: How do you feel?
CLAY: Good.
ANGIE: That's good.
CLAY: Dizzy.
ANGIE: That'll be the oxygen.
CLAY: How's Pop?
ANGIE: Pop?
CLAY: I left him with you.
ANGIE: Er—
CLAY: How long have I—
ANGIE: Three days.
CLAY: Days?
ANGIE: You gave us a scare.

CLAY: I did?
ANGIE: What's a bonefish?
CLAY: Sorry?
ANGIE: You were having a nightmare.
CLAY: [*remembering*] Keithen!
ANGIE: Shhh. Relax, he's fine.
CLAY: And Isaiah?
ANGIE: Isaiah as well.

    CLAY *sinks back, eyes closed, in thanks.*

  He's a character.
  Your pop.
  You had him listed next of kin.
CLAY: … How is he?
ANGIE: You should call him.
CLAY: Why?
ANGIE: Are you hungry? I can get you a drink, if you like? I think there's a tap in here somewhere.
CLAY: How'd they get out?
ANGIE: Sorry?
CLAY: Keithen and Isaiah.
ANGIE: …
CLAY: Ange …
ANGIE: You need to rest
CLAY: What I need is you to tell me the truth.
ANGIE: We almost lost you all right!
  If I hadn't found you when I did …
  Look, I'm sorry.
  But there was nothing you could do.

END OF ACT ONE

ACT TWO: RAPTURE

SCENE EIGHTEEN: O_2

SFX: someone on oxygen, the breathing is shallow.

CLAY: We sit in the living room, nursing cold cups of tea. TV's on, but no-one's watching. Small talk attempted and abandoned at the slightest noise from Pop's room.

Aunty Kim goes in to check on him. Through the door I hear him gasping. He hasn't eaten in weeks. She gives him water, but it hurts too much to swallow. She turns his pillow, lays a flannel on his forehead and smooths Vaseline over the cracks in his lips. Asks him does he want anything?

He lost his wife thirty years ago, then a decade later his only daughter. Then went the hip, now the lungs, and yet his body refuses to die. World War Two couldn't kill him. Nothing can. Even when his mind's made up, his ragged body clings to life.

She holds his hand and talks about heaven, where he'll see Nan again and Mum, and he tells her he doesn't believe in that stuff, and she pretends not to hear him. Later he'll beg her to get Lil to shelter, before the bombing starts, and she'll tell him his little girl is safe, and there are no bombs now, and finally, relenting, yes, we're all in the shelter now.

She stays with him until he falls asleep, then, exhausted, tiptoes back to her bedroom to snatch a couple of hours rest, while me and Angie—

ANGIE: Another cuppa?
CLAY: I might go for a drive.
ANGIE: Okay.
  Don't you want to see him?
CLAY: Sure.
ANGIE: I mean, we came all this way.

CLAY: Watch him through the doorway. Head sunk in a pillow. Mouth open. A tuft of hair poking out of his pyjamas, as his chest rises and falls. His lungs are still working, barely, but he looks like a—

ANGIE: Clay?
CLAY: Yeah?
ANGIE: I just wondered—
    If you'd given any thought to what we—
CLAY: Not yet.
ANGIE: Oh.
CLAY: I mean, I haven't decided.
ANGIE: That's okay.
CLAY: I will.
ANGIE: It's just—
CLAY: Hungry?
ANGIE: Sorry?
CLAY: I'll grab some things for dinner.
ANGIE: Clay!
    You're a good man
    and I think you'd make / a good—
CLAY: I still haven't decided.
ANGIE: But you will.
CLAY: Back soon.

SCENE NINETEEN: CHASM

CLAY: Late afternoon, the sun already slanting, and the car park is empty. I pull up, grab my dive bag, and crunch up the gravel. The boards are still wet, the water warm underfoot, last footprints of the day's last divers. The wooden walkway cuts through the reeds and out onto the water, falters, hits a pontoon, and beyond are the ponds. I watch a heron stalking eels in the reeds. See a fox trot quickly through the marshes carrying something small and soft and grey in its mouth. I haven't been back here in twenty-three years, not since the night with Jess. Not since Mum left.

Unzip my bag and lay my gear on the boards: regulator; one tank of air plus a pony as backup; BCD; weights; fins; mask and snorkel;

compass and map; knife and torch; spare batteries and a handful of glowsticks. Working quickly in the day's last light I assemble my gear, secure tank to BCD, test the regulator— [*sucking in his breath*], check air—Green. Two-forty bar—then lay it down by the ladder while I slip on wetsuit and weights. Then, kneeling, take it up, enjoying the weight on my shoulders, then ease over to the edge of the jetty to slip on fins and mask and snorkel. Then stand, with the help of the handrail, looking down at my reflection, watch it scatter and school. I wait until the breeze drops off and the pond is still as glass, then pinch the nose, hold the mask, and step off the jetty, falling right through—

SFX: The sound of Clay breathing through a regulator.

And the water is warmer than I expect and colder than I remember, as I plunge, feet-first, like a nail, towards the bottom, then kick towards the surface, head back, carried up by the air in my lungs, tank and vest, mask breaking the surface like sunlight. I push my head back, watching the water run backwards, and behind it the reeds, now reversed, pushing down on the sky. Then slip below the surface, body twisting, curling back on itself like a comma unsprung.

The first pond is the smallest, only ten metres deep, and I reach its centre in a few dozen kicks. I hang there, silhouette against the sky, looking down through diagonals of light. The bottom still cloudy from the day's dives, a rolling fog stirred up from below. Fish dart in and out of shadow, scales glinting in the godlight. Catch my breath, then kick towards the opposite bank, find the channel through the reeds, careful not to touch the bottom, and then I'm through.

Abruptly, the earth opens up, the pond floor falling away beneath me—a sudden plunge of forty metres or more. High above, I hover over the canyon, caught like a sparrow in the eye of an eons-old storm; limestone hollowed out by centuries to form this breach in bone, the chasm calling out to me, bright fissure in the earth. Last look at the sun, then pull the dump valve—whoosh!—and then it's downward dog and duck dive under, hands and head first, down, down into the abyss.

The sky falls silent; gone the honking of geese and shriek of galahs replaced by a glassy stillness, the water thick with muffled sound. Underneath, plants ten or twelve-foot-tall stretch towards the sun, bodies caught in unseen currents, light dancing on the leaves. As the water deepens, it darkens; chasm walls closing in. At ten metres, check the dial. The weight of two atmospheres already putting the squeeze on me. Even at this level, a full tank of gas only lasts half as long. Because the deeper you go, the more air it takes to fill your lungs, and every pull on the reg drops the needle lower. What did Jock call it? Dying by degrees. With every exhalation you give up a little more of the life left inside.

At thirty metres on the edge of the dark zone, I switch on my torch, find an anchor point and tie off my reel, then loosen the locknut, playing it out behind me like a kite string. I'm sinking fast now, check the watch, adjust buoyancy. At forty metres the tunnel doglegs, chasm narrowing to a shaft, then drops another fifteen before it hits the saddle. I pull up beside it, a rough outcrop caught like a fishbone in the sinkhole's throat. Take a moment to rest, check my air, then turn my back on sky and slip down past the saddle, down the wishing well, stone walls closing in. Push down face-first, no turning back now, even if I wanted to, darkness calling me deeper, hand over hand, until my fingers strike sand. Columns of clay rise like smoke. And then this great cloud of silt billows up like a nebula, browning everything out.

That was dumb. Dunno know what I thought I'd find down here, but this isn't it. Check the dial before the silt obscures it. One-seventy bar. Almost orange. Time to go. Thank God for the line. Catch my breath, and then—

SFX: Music. Coldplay. Faint.

Mum?

Silt blooms
like a bruise all around me.
Torchlight strangled,
the water
dim and dark as pewter.

Trace my fingers,
slide them under the sand
until my wrists plunge through.
Then dig down
through mud soft as satin,
hands scooping sludge,
dredging fistfuls of ooze.
And the music's getting louder
clearer.
Reach down towards it,
so close I can touch the notes
but something's holding me back.
Look around.
Catch the last light
glinting off the gold line
then
back at the reel.
Sixty metres.
As far as I go.
Look back above,
then down below.
Press my ear to the mud.
Listening.
But already the music is fading.
Reach around
for the line.
Find the knife
and I'm free.

Push down through the pain, hollowing it out, burrowing down beneath the mud like a worm. Braille diving now, chasing coldwater currents, pushing down through silt and sand and stone, until I'm through.

SCENE TWENTY: UNDERWORLD

CLAY: Darkness, total and unending.
Yet even without eyes I can sense it,
the vastness of it
stretching on forever,
infinite ocean under a sunless sky.
And the water cold and black as lacquer as I fall,
like a comet into endless night.
This must be what it was like.
Back before God threw the switch
and set the void alight.
And this down here
is all that's left
of all that was.
Last drop
of ink
spilled down
through
cracks
in the earth
diesel dark and full of—

    CLAY *stops.*

You feel that?

    CLAY *reaches his fingers out, feeling the water, eyes tight, sensing for something.*

I thought—
Ha!
Keep it together mate.
That's the nitrogen talking.
No-one else down here but us.

    Beat.

    He snaps a glowstick.

See!

ACT TWO

He checks his depth gauge and air levels, whistles.

Time to go.
At least the spare should see me—

He drops the glowstick.

Watch it fall,
end over end,
like hands on a clock
running backwards,
counting down,
to what I don't know,
till it's barely a blip
and the bonefish takes it.
This great shadow
rushing it
taking it whole
like a lure.
And
in that second before it swallows the light
I know
what it is,
this thing
that's been hunting me my whole life.
I can feel it.
Hurtling towards me
eyes like headlights
and there's nothing I can do now
but—

He starts to sing, the first line of 'Yellow' by Coldplay.

He stops.

It hits like a truck.
The force of it
wrenching bone,
punching air from my lungs.
And then the bonefish takes me down.

SCENE TWENTY-ONE: XIBALBA

Liquid black.

CLAY startles awake. A great inrush of breath!

CLAY: Aaaaahhhhhhhhhhhh

    Then out.

Her

aah

her

aah

her
aah

her

    Shivering.

Deep water blackouts.
Brain
starting to fizz.
Snap, crackle and
Pop

    CLAY giggles.

Can you hear that?
…
The ground feels
crunchy.
Slips and shifts
as I crawl.
Fishbones.
Others too.

ACT TWO

Stray cats
cows
and sheep that took a tumble
and underneath
there are
skulls
big as engine blocks,
megafauna dreaming.

   SFX: A heartbeat, almost imperceptible.

The tank is empty.
Push off
from the bottom.
The ground
oddly yielding.
Then drift
through the dark
on the lung's last breath,
holding on
as long as it will take me.

***

It starts at the edges.
Tunnel vision.
The mind shutting down.
Sparks dance in my eyes.
And I'm grateful
for this last gift of light.
The water warm and dark as claret.
Coming home now.
Then something
bumps me in the—

A body?
Tangled in line.
Hands outstretched,
fingers nibbled to bone.

I turn him gently.
The wetsuit, old rubber,
eyes blue, like my own.
My brother,
Moss.
Is that you?

He floats
like a candle
like Christ.
His body gone to soap.
Touch my forehead to his.
Whisper thanks.
Unhook
the tank on his back.
Connect reg.
Open valve
and
breathe.

Aaaaaaahh!

Then
up
towards the stars.

> *LX: A soft glow from above. SFX: A soft Coldplay refrain.*

She floats.
Knees drawn to her chest.
Ankles grasped in her hands.
Her body in a ball.
Weightless and waiting.
She drifts
down towards me
like a slow falling star.

Mum?

The word slips out
before I catch it.
Tiny bubble of hope.
It billows up towards her,
fleet as quicksilver.
See it catch
on her clavicle.
And her eyelids
flutter.
And there it is,
the truth.
Not drowned, then,
Dreaming.
All these years on her own.

Mum, it's me.
...
Her eyes open.
And her body unfolds
like a flower.
Pale
and naked as a fish.
Mum?
I've come to bring you home.

And you smile.
And that's when you show me.

SCENE TWENTY-TWO: LAST BREATH

A small reflection of light overhead.

CLAY: There
    See it?
    Tiny glimmer of light.
    Up above.
    The one you missed.

The one you never saw.
Only this time it's different,
because I'm here.
Both of us
swimming up together.
We link hands
kick away from the darkness
chasing light
until my fingers touch stone.

The gap
is whisper thin.
Just a pinprick of light.
Trace the line with my finger.
Chip away at it
like a chick at its egg.
Then the dive knife.
Scrimshawing home.
Feel it deepen and widen
until my whole hand is through.
And now the other.
Both hands hunting for purchase
as I hang like a bat
in this pillar of light.

Woohoo!

And Mum.
She looks
like an angel
Skin luminous.
And her eyes
iridescent.

And your smile.
Fuck, I almost forgot.

You're not coming,
are you?
…
I know.
…
But you know
I can't stay.

She kisses me
once
on each eyelid.
…
And when I open my eyes
…
Time to wake up.
One last look
then ease my way up,
up the chimney,
arms and elbows
lifting me.
First the head
then the shoulders.
Tunnelling north
out of Erebus.
Metre
by metre.
Slow and steady.
From night into day.
And all it takes is a lifetime.
And I'm almost through.
One last push

then
the dive tank
catches.

Push
back down.
Try again
but the tank's too big.
Edge back out.
Unzip vest,
shrug it off,
detach the tank
and push the bottle through first.
Then pull up behind it,
first one arm
then the head.
Second shoulder
tucked in tight.
Then the ribs.
And it's got me.
Try to pull myself through,
take a second.
But there's not enough purchase.
Try again.
And once more
but it's useless
fingernails scrabbling.
No choice then.
Breathe everything out
void the lungs
and
squeeeeeeeeeeeeeeeeeeeeeezzzzzzzzzzzzzzzzzzze
but my hips.
Try to push
but the torch
on my belt.
And I'm jammed
like a cork in a bottle.
I can see it.
A perfect circle of light
up above.

ACT TWO

Watch it shimmer and dance.
And I'm so bloody close!
Close my eyes
and let go.

JOCK: Fucksake.
CLAY: Hello?
Jock? Is that you?
JOCK: Mate, what are you doing down there?
CLAY: I think I'm dying.
JOCK: What do you want to do that for?
CLAY: I'm stuck.
JOCK: Well figure it out. There's people counting on you.
CLAY: Who?
JOCK: Who?

CLAY: And he laughs. And I see them …

Ben and Bridget, come over to ask if I can play. And Ian Marshall from Acacia Court, and all the kids at Scouts; and Mrs Searle, my old maths teacher, who never gave up on me. And there beside her is Catherine, who I had my first kiss with, and Jess in Melbourne now, and Freya, still in Thailand, still dancing to Da Rude. And there's Dev and Dan and Aditi, still bickering over cards and urging me to play with them—go on—one more round. And Alessandro, awake now, rubbing sleep from his eyes. And there's Baahir spotwelding and bugger me if the weld isn't straight and true and the most perfect thing you ever saw. And—hey!—there's Keithen, back on his feet, none the wiser, still acting the fool and Jock pretending to throttle him—both of them play-acting—now Jock's forgiven him for dying and breaking all our hearts. And isn't that Jacques Cousteau! And Harold Holt beside him, but no-one seems to recognise him, only me, and Harold winks! And then I see Pop in his uniform, a dozen medals glinting, hair Brylcreemed and black, face young and unlined like a matinee idol. And there beside him is Angie, and she's glowing, and there, cradled in her arms, lies my little baby girl. And I can't stay now, because a kid needs her dad, and I won't let her down. I draw breath then push—Hngngngg—with everything I've got until—

SNAP!
My ribs pop like fireworks.
First one,
then
two,
three,
four!
The pain of it shocking me awake. Drop back down through the gap to Mum and Moss and all that's underneath to say goodbye, then unbuckle weight belt and torch, one last breath from the reg, then, leaving it, slip like an eel through the roof and leave this hollow world behind.

SCENE TWENTY-THREE: CATHEDRAL

CLAY: Rising fast now,
    lungs expanding,
    and all the air that's left in me
    lifting me
    in one long exhale
    and all that's left is light.
    Everything brighter.
    More radiant.
    The water
    phosphorescing
    and flaring,
    birthing galaxies
    behind me.
    Fish
    zip past
    like comets
    And time too
    Rushing onwards
    then curving back on itself
    in an endless arcing wave.

    I hear the sound before I see it
    Deep bass resounding

The shockwave lifting me up
Then smashing me down.

Push up
past riverweed
and tanglewood,
roach and sturgeon,
their eyes unblinking
bodies ripped apart by tracer rounds
and the night is on fire.
Watch it roll across the surface
lighting the river up.
Every snag and every hollow
and then …

At first
I think it's a cross.
Not a cross,
but a plane,
slow falling,
wings outstretched,
propellor down.

And there!
A figure
dragged behind it,
just a boy
knocked out of the sky.

Swim up towards him.
And the terror
in his eyes.
And below me
the bonefish is stirring.
Try to warn him
but too late.
Watch it rise

from the deep
slow and certain as fate.
Come to snap him up
and take him down
to Mum and Moss below.

Only this time I'm faster.
HEY UGLY!
And with a flick of its tail,
it charges towards me,
eyes rolling back in its head
jaws springing open
like a trap
as I thrust the knife
deep in its gills.
Bonefish thrashing,
wrenching its head back and forth
trying to loose me,
but I hold on tight to the pain,
ride it up towards him,
then let go
kick away
to the boy,
grabbing hold of his foot,
cut it loose
as his young eyes widen,
and now the two of us are rising through the water,
me and Pop
up,
up,
up,
towards
the memory of light.

THE END

STATE THEATRE COMPANY SOUTH AUSTRALIA AND COUNTRY ARTS SA IN
ASSOCIATION WITH FLINDERS UNIVERSITY PRESENT

CATHEDRAL
BY CALEB LEWIS

CAST & CREATIVE TEAM

PLAYWRIGHT	Caleb Lewis
DIRECTOR	Shannon Rush
SET & COSTUME DESIGNER	Kathryn Sproul
LIGHTING/VIDEO DESIGNER	Mark Oakley
SOUND DESIGNER/COMPOSER	Andrew Howard
ASSISTANT DIRECTOR	Zola Allen
CLAY	Nathan O'Keefe
ANGIE	Anna Steen
JOCK	Chris Pitman
KEITHEN	Arran Beatie
JESS	Annabel Matheson
WILL/TED/SUPER	Rory Walker
DJ/DEV/DAN	AJ Pate
TOPSIDE	Gavin Norris
ADITI	Sandra Anderson
PRODUCTION MANAGER	Gabrielle Hornhardt
STAGE MANAGER	Bridget Samuel
TOURING TECHNICIAN	Abbie Heuer
TOURING TECHNICIAN	Tom Bayford

Costumes made by State Theatre Company South Australia Wardrobe.
Set constructed by State Theatre Company South Australia Workshop.
Cover Image: Richard Harris

Ngadlu tampinthi Kaurna miyurna yaitya yarta-mathanya Wama Tarntanyaku. Parnaku yailtya, parnaku tapa purruna, parnaku yarta ngadlu tampinthi. Yalaka Kaurna Miyurna itu yailtya, tapa purruna, yarta kuma puru martinthi, puru warri-apinthi, puru tangka martulayinthi. Ngadlu tampinthi purkarna pukinangku, yalaka, tarrkarritya.

We acknowledge the Kaurna people as the traditional custodians of the Adelaide Plains. We recognise and respect their cultural heritage, beliefs and relationship with the land. We acknowledge that they are of continuing importance to the Kaurna people living today and pay respects to Elders past, present and future.

WRITER'S NOTE - CALEB LEWIS

Seventy metres down the world falls away. First reds, then oranges, yellows, greens, and blues, until there's nothing but the night. Next goes touch, as your fingers go numb, the water wicking the heat away from you, and then all that's left to imagine is memory and sound.

When I was ten, on a family road trip from Melbourne to Adelaide, I first encountered the underworld. I remember the reeds and the low hanging sky, and dad pulling on his wetsuit in the carpark as he told us about all the people who'd died here. Piccaninnie Ponds is a system of sinkholes on South Australia's limestone coast, just south of Mt Gambier. The "Pics" are a mecca for divers the world over, drawn by tales of crystal-clear water; yawning chasms; and a vast underwater cathedral flooded with godlight. Dad was a dive instructor, not a licenced cave diver, but he was here, he figured, and the chance might never come again. We trailed up the wooden walkway behind him and waited as he slipped on his dive mask and flippers. Then he called us close and kissed us on the forehead – won't be long, he said – then he slipped beneath the surface. And I wondered what happens if he never comes back?

Cathedral is a play about a diver still haunted by loss, still lost in the deep and the dark. It asks why do some of us sink when others swim? What draws us down into the dark and what calls us back into the light?

In 2020, like so many others, I fell down a pretty dark hole. On top of the uncertainty of Covid and the seeming death of democracy, we lost my Uncle Jeff, then Uncle Julian, and then, impossibly, Logan, just a boy of barely fourteen. I liken depression to a well, and much of my life has been spent clinging to the stones, halfway down, just holding on. Sometimes it's easier to let go, hit rock-bottom and catch my breath before the slow climb back to the surface. But this year was harder, the bottom felt colder, darker, and the sky so far away. It's where I wrote this play. It is a thing steeped in grief, yet ultimately about finding our way back into the light. And if you are down there right now, know that night is only fleeting, that you are not alone, and when you are ready, the world is waiting and alive with light.

For Lucas, Heath, and Logan.

Caleb

Thank you to all at State Theatre Company South Australia and Country Arts SA for commissioning this new work, Mitchell Butel for championing it; Shannon Rush for so ably shepherding it; and Nathan O'Keefe for so richly bringing its world to life. Thanks also to Andrew Howard for his powerful soundscape; and Kathryn Sproul and Mark Oakley for their exquisite design. Huge thanks are also due to divers, Dr. Richard Harris; Josh Richards; Darren Mitchell; and Ian Lewis (Louie) and Peter Horne (Puddles) for sharing their knowledge and experience of a hidden world beneath our own. Thank you also to Suzie Miller, Aunty Michelle; District Ranger Ross Anderson; Graham Kilsby, Sarah Brokensha; Bridget Samuel; Louisa Norman; Keith Frost; my agents Emma and Monica at MKM; and lastly to Tim O'Brien, whose brilliant *The Things They Carried* inspired the play's ending.

Piccaninnie Ponds. Image: Caleb Lewis.

PLAYWRIGHT
CALEB LEWIS

Caleb is a multi-award-winning playwright, theatremaker and experience designer.

Plays for the stage include *Nailed, Clinchfield, Dogfall, Death in Bowengabbie, Rust and Bone, Songs for the Deaf, Aleksander and the Robot Maid, The Honey Bees, In a Dark Dark Wood, Six Million Hits, Men, Love and the Monkeyboy, The River at the End of the Road, Maggie Stone, Transcendence* and *Destroyer of Worlds*.

Games, installations and interactive entertainments include *Across a Crowded Room, Half an Hour Visit, If There Was A Colour Darker Than Black I'd Wear It, Tin Shed Camping Tours, Exclusion Zone, A Little History Play* and *Unkiss Me*.

Caleb was mentored by Nick Enright *(Blackrock, Lorenzo's Oil)* and Edward Albee *(Who's Afraid of Virginia Woolf?)* and is the winner of an Inscription Award, the Company B Belvoir Phillip Parsons Award (in absentia), an Australian Writer's Guild Award for Digital Narrative, and the inaugural Richard Burton Award for New Plays.

His work has been commissioned and/or produced by Griffin Theatre (NSW), Black Swan State Theatre Company (WA), Brisbane Festival, Bell Shakespeare (national), Hothouse (Vic), Sport for Jove (NSW) and State Theatre Company South Australia. He is currently completing a doctorate on ephemeral encounters and dynamic narrative at the nexus of theatre and games.

DIRECTOR
SHANNON
RUSH

Shannon is a professional theatre director, holding an Advanced Diploma in Acting from the Adelaide College of the Arts (2003) and a Bachelor of Creative Arts in Directing with First Class Honours from Flinders University (2016). Shannon also trained at the Trinity Laban Conservatoire of Music and Dance (London 2004) with funding assistance from the Helpmann Academy.

In 2022 Shannon will direct two new educational puppet shows written by Julianne O'Brien and commissioned by Camp Quality. She is also working on creative developments including *Starweaver* with Madness of Two Productions, and *WEIGHT* with Jasmin McWatters.

Shannon's directing credits include *Wolfgang's Magical Musical Circus* (Tour Director) for Circa Contemporary Circus, *Claire Della and The Moon* (Madness of Two Productions) and *Limit* by Sophia Simmons for State Theatre Company South Australia's 2019 Umbrella program. Shannon worked as Assistant Director on the Auckland Arts Festival tour of *1984* (GWB Entertainment) as well as the Australian tour (State Theatre Company South Australia).

In 2016, she directed the world premiere of Duncan Graham's play *Red Ink* for the Adelaide Fringe, and Rainer Werner-Fassbinder's *Pre-Paradise Sorry Now* for Adelaide College of the Arts. In the same year, she also worked as Assistant Director to Rosemary Myers on *Rumpelstiltskin* for Windmill Theatre Co and State Theatre Company South Australia, and to David Mealor on *The Juliet Letters* for Adelaide Cabaret Festival. As part of her Honours year studies at Flinders University she worked on secondment with Gale Edwards on the world premiere of *Cloudstreet* for Opera SA. Shannon also worked extensively with Oval House Theatre in London between 2004-2009 as a freelance director.

SET & COSTUME DESIGNER
KATHRYN SPROUL

Kathryn designs nationally for theatre, opera, dance and large arts events. Projects include *The Appleton Ladies' Potato Race* and *Gorgon* (State Theatre Company South Australia); *Glengarry Glenross, True West, The Dark Room* and *Seawall* (Flying Penguin Productions), *Limit* (Shannon Rush Productions for State Theatre Company South Australia's Umbrella program), *Gynt, Anatomy of A Suicide, Julius Caesar, Birdland, Love & Information, The Art of War, Arden versus Arden* and *Punk Rock* (Flinders University SA), *Can You Hear Colour* (Patch Theatre), *Sons & Mothers* (No Strings Attached), *Muckheap* (Polyglot Puppet Company, touring Shanghai & Australia), *The Flood* (Finucane & Smith/Critical Stages, national tour), Costume Designer for *Maria de Buenos Aires* (Leigh Warren & Dancers/Vic Opera).

Major event designs include the memorable *Flamma Flamma: The Fire Requiem* for 1998 Adelaide Festival of Arts, *Click! The Millennium Event* - SA's 1999 New Year's Eve Celebration and Event Development and Design for Centenary of Federation South Australia 2001.

Festival Event Design includes Adelaide Cabaret Festival 2005-2011 and 2016-2018, OzAsia Festival and Moon Lantern Parade 2007-2014 and Adelaide International Guitar Festival 2007-2014.

Venue design includes the award-winning Queens Theatre, Adelaide Fringe 2012.

Film and television credits include set design for *Talking Heads* and *Poh's Kitchen* (ABC), Channel Nine Women's and Children's Hospital Easter Appeal, 2015 and 2016.

A graduate in Stage Design from NIDA, Kathryn was Resident Designer for Magpie Theatre and State Theatre Company South Australia from 1988-1993. Kathryn has worked with other companies including Patch Theatre, Vitalstatistix, Cirkidz, Legs on The Wall, Playbox, Chamber Made Opera, Hothouse, Melbourne Theatre Company, Red Stitch, NORPA, The Production Company, Adelaide Festival of Arts, Adelaide Fringe Festival, Brisbane Festival and Qld Music Festival.

LIGHTING/ VIDEO DESIGNER
MARK OAKLEY

Mark Oakley is 6'5 and is not British. He is a technical designer and manager working on Kaurna Yerta and the world.

His most recent designs include *Clock for No Time and Blood, Sweat and Karaoke* (RUMPUS), *Gynt: After Ibsen* (Flinders Drama Centre), *Claire Della and the Moon* (Madness of Two), *Limit* (State Theatre Company South Australia's Umbrella production), *30,000 Notes* (Under the Microscope), *The Executioners* (Anya Anastasia) and *Phantom of the Opera* (GASSA).

He has spent numerous years touring with Slingsby Theatre Company *(The Young King, Emil and The Detectives)* and continued travelling up to Woodford Folk Festival, where he was responsible for set electrical effects.

Mark spent the 2018 Fringe season as resident lighting designer for *The Lab at Queens Theatre* and has also spent several years working at Co Opera during which designed and toured several shows interstate *Cosi Fan Tutte* (2015), *Magic Flute* (2015). Mark graduated from Brighton Secondary School in 2011.

SOUND DESIGNER/ COMPOSER
ANDREW HOWARD

Andrew is Resident Sound Designer for State Theatre Company South Australia.

His sound design credits for State Theatre Company South Australia include *Girls & Boys, Who's Afraid of Virginia Woolf?, Hibernation, The Appleton Ladies' Potato Race, Euphoria, The Boy Who Talked to Dogs* (with Slingsby Theatre), *Ripcord, Gaslight, Dance Nation, Jasper Jones, End of the Rainbow, Animal Farm, The Gods Of Strangers, That Eye, The Sky, Terrestrial, After Dinner, In The Club, Vale, Macbeth, A Doll's House, 1984* (Australian Associate Sound Designer), *Sista Girl, Machu Picchu, This Is Where We Live, Kryptonite, Maggie Stone, Babyteeth, Random, The Kreutzer Sonata, Romeo and Juliet, Knives in Hens* and *Attempts On Her Life*.

His other theatre credits as Sound Designer and/or Composer credits include *Helly's Magic Cup, Grug, Nyuntu Ngali, Fugitive, School Dance, The Story Thieves* and *Girl Asleep* (Windmill Theatre Co), *Rumpelstiltskin* and *Pinocchio* (State Theatre Company South Australia/Windmill Theatre Co), *Despoiled Shore, Medeamaterial, Landscape with Argonauts, The War, Please Go Hop!, Highway Rock 'n' Roll Disaster, Trouble On Planet Earth* and *Disappearance* (The Border Project), *One Long Night in The Land of Nod* and *The Homecoming* (Floogle), *The Birthday Party* and *Blackbird* (Flying Penguin Productions), *Boxing Day Test* (Junglebean) and *Little Green Tractor* (Patch Theatre).

CLAY
NATHAN O'KEEFE

Nathan has worked extensively in theatre, both nationally and internationally. He has toured Asia, USA, and all across Australia, working for companies such as State Theatre Company South Australia, Sydney Theatre Company, Melbourne Theatre Company, Windmill Theatre, Griffin Theatre, Malthouse, Bell Shakespeare, Brink Productions and Slingsby.

Recent State Theatre Company South Australia credits include *Gaslight, Hydra* (with Queensland Theatre) *Sense and Sensibility, Macbeth, In The Club, A Doll's House, Tartuffe* (with Brink Productions), *Things I Know To Be True* (with Frantic Assembly), *The Importance of Being Earnest, Hedda Gabler* and *Masquerade* (State Theatre Company South Australia/Griffin), *Betrayal* (State Theatre Company South Australia/MTC) and the title role of *Pinocchio* (State Theatre Company South Australia/Malthouse/ STC/NY for the US premiere season at The New Victory Theatre on Broadway).

Other credits include *Talk to Me Like the Rain, Let Me Listen, Hot Fudge, Ghosts, King Lear, The Complete Works of William Shakespeare (Abridged)* and *Three Sisters* (State Theatre Company South Australia), *Thursday, The Hypochondriac, Harbinger* (Brink), *this uncharted hour* (State Theatre Company South Australia/ Brink Productions), *Man Covets Bird* (Slingsby), *I Am Not An Animal, I Animal* (The Border Project), *Mr. McGee and the Biting Flea, Emily Loves To Bounce, Me & My Shadow* (Patch), *Hiccup!, Plop!, Grug, Grug & The Rainbow* (Windmill Theatre Co), *Checklist for an Armed Robber, Ruby Bruise* (Vitalstatistix), *Assassins* (Flying Penguin) and *The Country and Blackout* (Stone/Castro).

Nathan is an Adelaide Theatre Guide and Adelaide Critics Circle Award recipient.

**STAGE MANAGER
BRIDGET SAMUEL**

Bridget graduated from Adelaide College of the Arts in 2008. Her Stage Management credits for State Theatre Company South Australia include *Who's Afraid of Virginia Woolf?*, *Hibernation*, *Euphoria*, *After Dinner*, *The Comedy Of Errors*, *In The Next Room (or The Vibrator Play)*, *Top Girls*, *The Glass Menagerie*, *The Ham Funeral* and *The Misanthrope*, and Assistant Stage Manager for *Summer of the Seventeenth Doll*, *The Complete Works of William Shakespeare (Abridged)* and *Maestro*. Bridget was also the props buyer for State Theatre Company South Australia's *The Memory of Water*, *Entertaining Mr Sloane* and *Girl from the North Country*.

Bridget toured nationally with *Henry V*, *Hamlet*, *Othello*, *The Merchant of Venice*, *Julius Caesar* and *Much Ado about Nothing* (Bell Shakespeare). She has also been part of the stage management team for *Moby Dick*, *La Sonnambula*, *Carmen*, *Hansel and Gretel*, *Pearl Fishers*, *Aida*, *Tales of Hoffman*, *Flying Dutchman*, *Girl of the Golden West* and *Rigoletto* (State Opera South Australia), *A Midsummer Night's Dream*, *Mozart's Requiem*, *Breaking the Waves*, *Two Feet*, *Zizanie*, *Le Grand Macabre* and *Mahler 8* (Adelaide Festival), *How Not to Make It in America* (Theatre Republic) and *Thursday* (Brink Productions).

**ASSISTANT DIRECTOR
ZOLA ALLEN**

Zola Allen is an Adelaide based actor, director and theatre maker. She studied at Adelaide College of the Arts in the Advanced Acting course, graduating in 2018.

Some highlights from her time at AC Arts include *Mercutio* in Nescha Jelk's *Romeo & Juliet*, Casca in *Julius Caesar* and Stan in her graduate show *Aftershocks*.

Since graduating, Zola has worked in the Adelaide indie theatre scene playing Guildenstern in *Rosencrantz and Guildenstern Are...* and as Linda the clown in the dark satirical comedy *Dead Gorgeous* presented (Madness of Two).

As well as performing, Zola has been part of show developments working with companies such as Vitalstatistix, FRANK theatre and Deus Ex Femina.

Zola co-founded the theatre company Good Company Theatre and recently made her directorial debut with *Hamlet in the Other Room*. Most recently she performed in *All the Things I Couldn't Say* directed by Katherine Sortini for Deus Ex Femina's 2022 Adelaide Fringe season.

State Theatre Company South Australia is the flagship theatre company of South Australia and is a resident artistic company of the Adelaide Festival Centre.

We commission, perform and tour theatrical productions of new and existing, classic and contemporary, Australian and international work. From a rich legacy of visionary theatre makers and landmark theatrical productions, we strive to make, present and promote phenomenal, transformative, and inclusive theatre that enriches South Australian and Australian culture.

We are also committed to a diversity of artistic voices (including First Nations and culturally and linguistically diverse voices) and audiences and access to all. State Theatre Company South Australia is committed to providing platforms and pushing boundaries and for being recognised for high quality and large-scale theatrical storytelling that has an eye to the sky but an ear to the ground.

STATE THEATRE
COMPANY SOUTH AUSTRALIA
statetheatrecompany.com.au

STATE THEATRE COMPANY SOUTH AUSTRALIA

BOARD

Amanda Anderson
Alexandra Dimos
Claudine Law
Jodie Newton
David O'Loughlin
Diané Ranck
Joe Thorp (Chair)
Gavin Wanganeen

FOUNDATION

Alexandra Dimos
Christine Guille
Anthony Keenan
Diané Ranck
Meredyth Sarah AM
Andrew Sweet (Chair)
Sarah Rohrsheim
Simon White

STAFF

EXECUTIVE

ARTISTIC DIRECTOR
Mitchell Butel

EXECUTIVE DIRECTOR
Julian Hobba

ARTISTIC

ARTISTIC PROGRAM MANAGER
Shelley Lush

RESIDENT DIRECTOR
Anthony Nicola

WRITERS UNDER COMMISSION
Samuel Adamson
Elena Carapetis
Anna Goldsworthy
Verity Laughton
Caleb Lewis
Meow Meow
Emily Steel
Alexis West

DATA & TICKETING

CRM AND TICKETING MANAGER
Emma Quinn

TICKETING SUPERVISOR
Rosie George

DEVELOPMENT & PHILANTHROPY

DEVELOPMENT MANAGER
Catherine Bauer

DEVELOPMENT & EVENTS COORDINATOR
Alyssa Fletcher

EDUCATION

EDUCATION PROGRAM MANAGER
Fiona Lukac

FINANCE & ADMINISTRATION

BUSINESS MANAGER
Natalie Loveridge

FINANCE OFFICER
Inez Raspoet

MARKETING & COMMUNICATIONS

HEAD OF MARKETING & COMMUNICATIONS
Kristy Rebbeck

MARKETING EXECUTIVE
Jessica Zeng

PUBLICIST
Sophie Potts

GRAPHIC DESIGN & CONTENT COORDINATOR
Rachel Bell

CREATIVE SERVICES ADVISOR
Matt Byrne

PRODUCTION & WORKSHOP

PRODUCTION MANAGER
Gavin Norris

DEPUTY PRODUCTION MANAGER
Gabrielle Hornhardt

WORKSHOP SUPERVISOR
Areste Nicola

LEADING HAND
Patrick Duggin

PROPS COORDINATOR
Stuart Crane

CARPENTER/METAL WORKER
Guy Bottroff

SCENIC ART
Sandra Anderson

HEAD OF SOUND/ RESIDENT SOUND DESIGNER
Andrew Howard

PROP SHOP
Robin Balogh

STAGE MANAGEMENT TRAINEE
Carmen Palmer

WARDROBE

HEAD OF WARDROBE & COSTUME MAKER
Kellie Jones

WARDROBE PRODUCTION SUPERVISOR/BUYER
Enken Hagge

SHOW SUPERVISOR & COSTUME MAKER
Martine Micklem

WIGS, MAKE-UP & COSTUME HIRE
Jana DeBiasi

Country Arts SA's vision is for the artists and communities of regional South Australia to thrive through engagement with the arts, and be recognised as valued contributors to the nation's cultural voice.

The arts are a lead contributor to the strength of our regional communities. They shape our culture, identity and economy, contribute to employment, tourism and education, and support good health, wellbeing and community cohesion. Our work produces ambitious and accessible arts experiences while empowering regional communities to create and interact with the arts as audiences, participants, artists and leaders.

We acknowledge that we live and create on the lands of the First Nations people of South Australia and pay our respects to Elders past and present.

COUNTRY ARTS SA LEADERSHIP TEAM

CHIEF EXECUTIVE/EXECUTIVE DIRECTOR
Anthony Peluso

ARTS AND CULTURE LEADER
Merilyn de Nys

SUSTAINABILITY LEADER
Michael Bloyce

ARTS CENTRES LEADER
Sussan Baldwin

MARKETING AND DEVELOPMENT LEADER
Kyra Herzfeld

HEAD OF PEOPLE
Jill Bolzon

FOR CATHEDRAL

EXECUTIVE PROGRAMMER
Louisa Norman

ASSOCIATE PRODUCER –
MOUNT GAMBIER
Marina Santoretto

STRATEGIC INITIATIVES PRODUCER
Sarah Knight

MARKETING AND PUBLICITY OFFICER
Diana Maschio

DIGITAL STRATEGIST
Jessica Costello

HEAD OF DESIGN
Jarren Gallway

CORPORATE MARKETING &
PUBLICITY OFFICER
Helene Sobolewski

IT'S YOUR TIME

Whether you're stepping up or making a change, why wait to get into a career you're passionate about?

With Flinders midyear entry, it's your time to gain the skills you need to reach your full potential.

Apply now for midyear entry.

Flinders.edu.au

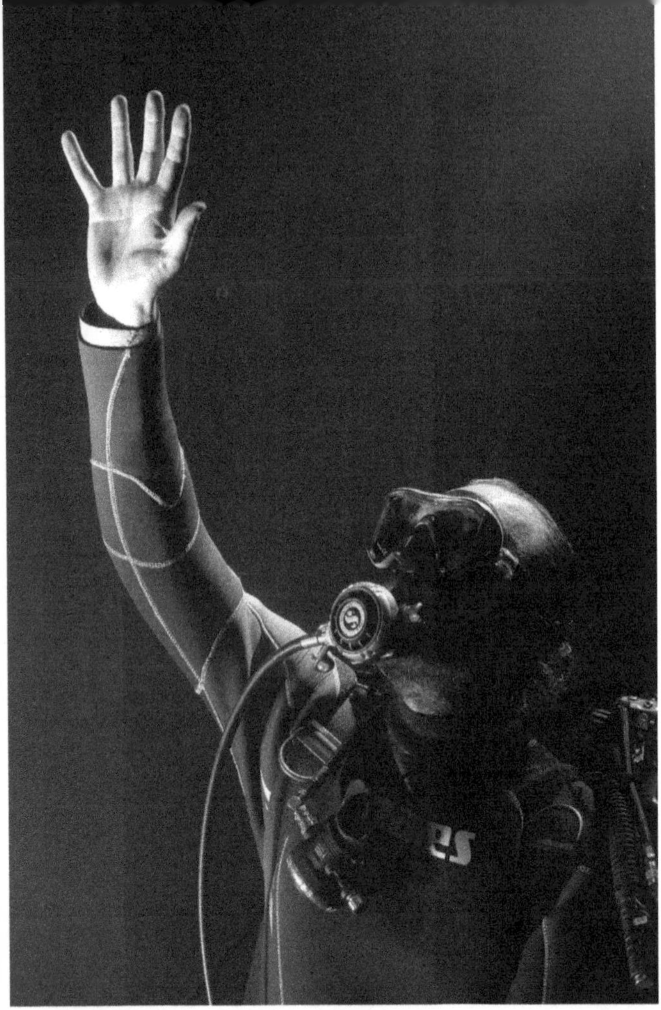

Left & Below: Nathan O'Keef
Photography: Jessica Zeng.

www.ingramcontent.com/pod-product-compliance
Lightning Source LLC
Chambersburg PA
CBHW050023090426
42734CB00021B/3396